101

Great Ways to Keep Your Child Entertained

While You Get Something Else Done

101

Great Ways to Keep Your Child Entertained

While You Get Something Else Done

DANELLE HICKMAN
AND
VALERIE TEURLAY

ST. MARTIN'S PRESS   NEW YORK

Design by Judith A. Stagnitto
Illustrations © 1992 Lizzy Rockwell

Library of Congress Cataloging-in-Publication Data

Hickman, Danelle.
    101 great ways to keep your child entertained while you get something else done / Danelle Hickman and Valerie Teurlay.
        p.   cm.
    Includes index.
    ISBN 0-312-07618-5
    1. Child rearing—United States.   2. Creative activities and seat work.   I. Teurlay, Valerie.   II. Title.   III. Title: One hundred and one ways to keep your child entertained.
HQ769.H55   1922
649'.51—dc20   92-3080
                                                                                        CIP

First edition: August 1992
10 9 8 7 6 5 4 3 2 1

Dedicated to our Mothers, who always said,
"Just wait until you have children of your own."

Contents

ACKNOWLEDGMENTS   xi
AUTHORS' NOTE   xiii
INTRODUCTION   xv

INDOOR PLAY

1. Fake Finger Painting   3
2. Indoor Sandbox   3
3. Bathtub Painting   4
4. Homemade Playdough   6
5. Play Kitchens   8
6. Cook's Assistant   9
7. Table Setting   10
8. Dishwashing   11
9. Housekeeping   11
10. Masking Tape Highways   12
11. Masks   13
12. Hand Puppets   14
13. Bean Bags   15
14. Life-size Doll   16
15. Paper Bag Blocks   16
16. Robot Play   17
17. Obstacle Course   18
18. Tent   19
19. Chalk   20
20. General Crayon   21
21. Crayon Rubbings   21
22. Magic Etchings   22
23. Resist Painting   22
24. Laundry Basket Play   23
25. Hair Salon   24

26.	Dress-up	25
27.	Dominoes	26
28.	Trampoline	27
29.	Stringing	28
30.	Puzzles	28
31.	Gluing Craft	29
32.	Sewing Cards	30
33.	Bake and Paint Sculpture	31
34.	Starch and Tissue Paper Collage	32
35.	Simple Scissor Craft	33
36.	Kiddie Correspondence	33
37.	Junk Mail	34
38.	Memory Book	35
39.	Personalized Photo Album	35
40.	Musical Instruments	36
41.	Homemade Cassette Tape	37
42.	Personalized Video	38
43.	Toy Pick-up Time	38

OUTDOOR PLAY

44.	Sidewalk Painting	41
45.	Chalk Graffiti	41
46.	Lawn Bowling	42
47.	Ice Castles	43
48.	Bubbles	44
49.	Water Play	45
50.	Toddler Boot Camp	46
51.	Tire Swings	47
52.	Grand Prix	48
53.	Under Construction	48
54.	Pit Stop	49
55.	Car Wash	49
56.	Butterfly Net	50
57.	Nature Collage	51
58.	Birdwatching	52

59. Rock Collecting   53
60. Hula Hoops   53
61. General Painting   54
62. Blow Painting   55
63. Roller Painting   56
64. Marble Painting   56
65. Stamp Painting   57
66. Sponge Painting   57
67. String Painting   58
68. Painted Spaghetti Art   58
69. Yard Work   59
70. Flower Garden   60
71. Magnet Magic   61
72. Picnic Lunch   62

AROUND TOWN

73. Personalized Road Map   65
74. Personalized Travel Tape   65
75. Toy Organizer   66
76. Travel Photo Album   66
77. Tour Guide   67
78. Cloth Activity Book   68
79. Sports Fan   69
80. Restaurant Dining   70
81. Grocery Shopping   70
82. Mall Shopping   71
83. Food to Go   72

SPECIAL OCCASIONS

84. Custom Birthday Invitations   75
85. Pretend Birthday Parties   75
86. Personalized Valentines   76
87. Easter Thumbprint Creatures   77
88. May Day Baskets   77

CONTENTS

89.	Mother's Day Jewelry	78
90.	Father's Day Tie	78
91.	Fourth of July Parade	79
92.	Haunted House	80
93.	Ghost	81
94.	Thanksgiving Indian Headdress	82
95.	Wrapping Paper Play	83
96.	Cookie Cutter Cards	83
97.	Holiday Wrapping Paper	84
98.	Tissue Paper Wreath	84
99.	Holiday Crayon Cookies	85
100.	Santa Play	86
101.	New Year's Eve Celebration	86

ACTIVITY INDEX 87
RECIPE INDEX 91

Acknowledgments

We wish to thank Cheryl Benner, Ruth Beyda, Patty Earhart, Esther Feldman, Gary Hickman, Shirley Hickman, Phyllis Kitagawa, Deborah Stone, Kim Straub, Dan Strauss, Harriet Strauss, Frank Teurlay, Adeline Weekly, and Mark Weekly for their help and guidance.

Special thanks to our husbands who made us mothers in the first place.

With gratitude to Judy Rothman and Sharon Tate who helped to make our book a reality.

Authors' Note

This book is geared for the 18-month to the 4-year-old child. Some of the activities are appropriate for the toddler, while others are for the preschooler. If you feel an activity is too advanced for your toddler, try it again at a later time.

You will find a clock next to each activity. The amount of time blocked out is approximately how long your child's attention may be held by the game or project. This time estimate will vary according to your child's age, personality, and developmental level. The clocks read as follows:

15 minutes   30 minutes   45 minutes   1 hour

The pronouns he and she have been used interchangeably throughout the book and are not intended to single out particular activities for one sex or the other.

There are both new and old ideas in this book. These have been collected from a variety of sources, tested, and refined. While we have found that the following 101 ideas promote creative, independent play, this book is in no way meant to be a replacement for the one-on-one attention a parent needs to give a child.

Important note to readers: Although this book is meant to stimulate independent play, the activities described require adult supervision and preparation. In addition to the usual safety measures taken when planning activities for young children, readers should note the safety precautions we have pointed out in boxes throughout the book.

Introduction

We're parents, too. We understand that time is precious—time to spend playing with your children and also time to do things for yourself, whether it's talking on the phone with a friend, or discussing the day's events with your spouse, or perhaps even reading something *you* want to read.

We've become firmly convinced that the best way to keep both parents and kids sane and happy is to find a balance between satisfying your children's needs and attending to your own. The question we kept asking ourselves was this: How can I find creative ways to keep my child entertained while freeing up a bit of time for myself?

Through trial and error—not to mention both wanted and unwanted advice from many people—we have learned it is possible to keep a child happily occupied. While you will still want to stay in close proximity to make sure your child is playing safely and to provide assistance when needed, this book focuses on activities that will help encourage INDEPENDENT PLAY by children ranging from the toddler period through the pre-school years.

The 101 activities in this book are organized into four thematic sections: Indoor Play, Outdoor Play, Around Town, and Special Occasions. We have attempted to choose activities that are simple and fun and that require minimal preparation time, and to cover most of the situations in which your child will want your attention. We hope the following ideas will work as successfully for you as they have for us and for our children, Elizabeth, Kelly, and Kimberly.

Indoor Play

1

Fake Finger Painting

For an edible and easy-to-clean method of indoor painting, allow your child to finger paint on a plastic cloth or cookie sheet with any of the following items: instant pudding, soft Jell-O, whipped cream, thick yogurt, or cooked cereal, such as oatmeal or Cream of Wheat.

2

Indoor Sandbox

Spread approximately 5 cups of graham cracker crumbs, Rice Krispies, or uncooked oatmeal on a large clean cookie sheet with sides or on a jelly roll pan. Your child will enjoy using small cars, spoons, or other kitchen utensils to make edible hills, roads, and sand cakes. This activity is great for the young toddler who puts everything in her mouth. A few more calories won't hurt, and the danger of swallowing inedible objects is eliminated.

3

Bathtub Painting

Your bathtub is an ideal spot for no-mess painting. Have your child temporarily transform the
inside of the tub into a mural with water-
soluble paint. When finished, turn on the water and wash
down both child and tub. See illustration.

Paint can be purchased at any toy or art supply store, or
the following recipe can be used.

▮ FINGER PAINT RECIPE ▮

½ cup cornstarch
1 cup cold water
1 envelope unflavored
  gelatin

2 cups boiling water
food coloring

Combine cornstarch and ¾ cup cold water in sauce pan. Mix well. Soak gelatin in ¼ cup cold water in separate dish and set aside. Add boiling water to cornstarch mixture, stirring as you pour. Cook over medium heat and stir constantly until boiling. When the mixture is thick and clear, remove from heat and stir in dissolved gelatin. When the mixture has cooled, divide it into separate containers for different colors. Then add a few drops of food coloring to each container, and mix.

Caution: Bathtubs are slippery.

4

Homemade Playdough

 Make playdough at home using the following recipe:

▌ PLAYDOUGH RECIPE ▌

1 cup flour
¹/₂ cup salt
2 teaspoons cream of tartar (spice)
1 cup water
1 tablespoon vegetable oil

Food coloring (for color) and peppermint oil or vanilla extract (for scent), or Kool-Aid (for color and scent)

After choosing items for color and scent, mix all the ingredients in a pan. Cook over a medium flame, stirring constantly. When the dough is very stiff, turn it onto a counter or table and knead it until it cools. Store your homemade playdough unrefrigerated in an air-tight container. It will keep for three months.

Give your child a small rolling pin or cylinder-shaped block and show him how to roll out the dough to a thickness into which the cookie cutters can be pressed.

Add some small pots and pans for cooking up pretend cakes, pies, spaghetti, or whatever your little chef wants to make the special of the day.

5

Play Kitchens

A child-size kitchen is a lifesaver. Your child will use it as a prop for his imagination and spend a great deal of time playing independently. If you have not yet invested in a play kitchen, a homemade stove and sink can be made from two large boxes.

Cut an oven door in one box and tape a piece of cardboard behind the burner area where accessories can be drawn. First paint or cover the box with paper to match the decor of his "house," then add other details such as burners, a clock, and a timer. Bolt on burner knobs and a handle to open the oven door—this can be done by making a hole in the cardboard, inserting a bolt, and then attaching a nut to hold it in place.

Make a kitchen sink out of the second large box and a plastic wash tub by cutting a hole in the top of the box

large enough for the tub to be dropped into. (Be careful not to make the hole too large, or the tub will fall through.) You can fill the play sink with water if the kitchen is used in a room without carpeting.

Your child will enjoy using real-life kitchen accessories such as empty margarine tubs, individual cereal boxes, empty spice tins, plastic spoons, and dishwashing utensils.

6

Cook's Assistant

You may often feel harassed by a demanding child when it's time to fix a meal. Occupy your child by allowing him to stir and pour ingredients. This activity is helpful for a picky eater, since he is more likely to eat food he is helping to prepare. While you continue your meal preparation, encourage your child to practice his pouring technique. Uncooked rice or dried peas can be easily poured from a pitcher into smaller containers by small children with a minimum of mess. Use water to practice measuring-cup activities. Example: pour 2 half-cups of water into 1 cup. Of course, it is best to limit these activities to the sink for easy cleanup.

Caution: Keep children away from a hot stove.

7

Table Setting

Your child will enjoy setting the table while you are busy preparing the meal. Set one place-setting as an example and allow your child to set the rest of the silverware and accessories.

Another way to teach your child to set a table properly is to allow him to make his own place mat. Purchase an inexpensive vinyl place mat and allow your child to trace around a place-setting with permanent markers. These place mats also make a great gift for grandparents.

Caution: No knives, please.

8

Dishwashing

Fill a sink with soapy water. Allow your child to play in the sink with plastic dishes, cups, spoons, vegetable scrubbers, sponges, and dishcloths. Soapsuds can be used to make pretend food such as cakes, mashed potatoes, or sodas. Make sure that your child is standing on a secure stool or chair, wearing a plastic apron or foul-weather jacket, and that the water is not too hot.

9

Housekeeping

Kids love to "help" when you're doing house-work. Allow your child to help with odd jobs such as shaking out laundry, carrying it to the appropriate room, and making the bed. Give your child a feather duster, an empty spray bottle, and cloth. There are also toys such as miniature brooms, irons, and sweepers available for imaginary housework.

10

Masking Tape Highways

Construct roads by rolling out wide masking tape on linoleum or tile floors. You can make straight roads, right- and left-hand turns, and intersections with the tape. Create a two-lane highway by drawing a line down the center of the road. Draw traffic signals, stop signs, and crosswalks on the tape. Create towns by using small boxes or toys such as houses, farms, gas stations, and miniature people. This is an entertaining way for your child to play with his transportation toys without running them over your toes every five minutes.

11

Masks

Children love to look into the mirror and pretend to see someone, or something, other than themselves. Encourage this kind of make-believe play by creating a simple mask. Using a medium-size paper bag or paper plate, cut out eyes, a nose, and/or a mouth. Create hair or mustache with yarn. Color, paint, or paste on any other features desired. The paper bag mask goes on over the head. Glue a popsicle stick at the base of a paper-plate mask for use as a handle. A favorite hat will add the finishing touch.

12

Hand Puppets

Puppets can be made from old socks and used over and over again. Paste or sew on felt and yarn for hair and facial features. Your child will readily entertain herself or a friend by putting on puppet shows. You also will have found a use for those socks that mysteriously lose their mates in the wash.

13

Bean Bags

Old socks never die, they become bean bags. Make simple bean bags by pouring dried beans or rice into old socks. Secure the bean bag by knotting the open end. The bean bags can be tossed back and forth, into containers, or through holes in a propped up piece of cardboard.

HAND PUPPETS

14

Life-size Doll

Create a life-size doll by tracing around your child's body while he is lying on a double layer of butcher paper. Cut out both layers of the silhouette and staple them together, leaving openings for the stuffing. Have your child paint or color a face on the doll which, with the help of crumpled newspaper stuffing, will bring the doll to life. Finish by stapling the doll closed all around. Since the doll and your child are approximately the same size, he will enjoy dressing his new buddy in his own clothes. This activity can help him to learn to dress himself.

15

Paper Bag Blocks

Make large blocks by firmly stuffing crumpled newspaper into paper grocery bags or cardboard boxes. Fold and tape the ends to give the bag block a firm, rectangular shape. Your child will enjoy using these blocks for climbing and stacking, or as part of an indoor obstacle course (see activity #17).

16

Robot Play

Remove the bottom of an appropriate-size box, and create a robot body by cutting holes for a head and arms. Your child can customize her costume by coloring, painting, or pasting objects on the box. For a high-tech look, cover the box with aluminum foil before decorating.

17

Obstacle Course

When the weather will not permit outdoor play, help your child release pent-up energy by building an obstacle course, using any of the following items:

- Pillows
- Mats
- Boxes
- Chairs
- Paper Bag Blocks (see activity #15)
- Balancing boards (wide planks of wood elevated off the floor with telephone books at each end)

Use these items as ramps, slides, tunnels, and bridges.

18

Tent

⬤ Your child may need his own little area "to get away from it all." Create a tent for him to hide in by placing a sheet or blanket over a table or two chairs. Make a bed out of blankets, sheets, pillows, or a sleeping bag. With the addition of several of your child's favorite stuffed animals for a little companionship, the tent becomes a cozy retreat. Even the child who dislikes taking naps can be coaxed into the tent for an occasional sleepy visit with his animal friends.

19

Chalk

Chalk is a good introduction to drawing for the younger child. Toddlers are often tempted to draw wherever they want. If you use chalk, which can be easily wiped off, you can spare your walls; it's also a good idea to teach your child to draw only on paper. A high chair, with tray in place, is a good location for this activity.

This is also a good opportunity to encourage your child's pride in her artistic ability by designating a special area to display her masterpieces. Pick a bulletin board, refrigerator, or bedroom door, securing the artwork with masking tape or magnets since push-pins and tacks are dangerous to the 4-and-under set.

Caution: Toddlers can choke on small pieces of chalk if swallowed. We recommend using dustless chalk, which can be found in educational toy stores.

20

General Crayon

Save your walls by using washable crayons, and stress that drawing is to be done only on paper. If possible, use a child-size table and chairs when doing arts-and-crafts projects. Supply large coloring books or oversize paper so your child does not mar the table's surface. At this age, your child will enjoy coloring on blank paper as much as a coloring book. Consider recycling paper from the office: the back of yesterday's memo can be a blank canvas for your little Rembrandt!

A combination of the activities described in numbers 20 through 23 should occupy your child for about an hour.

21

Crayon Rubbings

Round up flat objects with interesting textures such as leaves, a piece of screen, or a piece of burlap. Place them between two pieces of paper and clip together. Have your child gently rub a crayon on the surface of the paper over and around the concealed object. As he continues rubbing, a picture will appear.

22

Magic Etchings

Let your child color on a piece of white paper, filling most of the area with bright colors. Next, have him cover the artwork with a layer of black crayon. When he etches a design into the black crayon layer with a plastic spoon or a popsicle stick, the bright colors of the bottom layer will show through.

23

Resist Painting

Have your child color on a white piece of paper. Mix a color wash (50 percent paint/50 percent water) for her to paint over the entire surface. The crayon design will resist the paint, giving the artwork an interesting look.

24

Laundry Basket Play

A laundry basket is a good household item to use in imaginary play. Your child can sit in the basket and pretend it is a car or train. It can also be used as a bed for dolls or stuffed animals. Hiding a surprise inside the basket, under a blanket or quilt, is also fun.

25

Hair Salon

 Children have a fascination with hair. Let your child play with any of the following items:

- Ribbons and hair ornaments
- Curlers and large clips
- Unbreakable mirror
- Unplugged blow dryer or toy blow dryer (a battery-operated toy dryer that makes noise is great!)

Your child can use dolls with brushable hair as the "stylishly coiffed" customers, or even a playmate or sibling, provided no scissors are at hand.

Caution: Do not include scissors in this activity. This is a good time to discuss the adverse effects of a child cutting his own hair.

26

Dress-up

Save old costume jewelry, shoes, purses, hats, wigs, ties, and other assorted accessories for dress-up play. Have a mirror handy for your child to admire her "grown-up" appearance. Always have a designated place or container for dress-up items so that your child doesn't think your closet is fair game.

27

Dominoes

Your preschooler will enjoy making and playing her own domino game. Cut heavy paper, cardboard, or a file folder into rectangles. Draw a line across the middle to form squares. Paste or draw on letters, colors, numbers, shapes, or animals that can be matched. For added protection and durability, cover the dominoes with a clear-seal lamination. (Buy this sticky transparent sheet at a stationery store and trim it with scissors to fit each domino.) This last step is best done by an adult. Make approximately 20 dominoes for a game with two players.

∎ DOMINO RULES ∎

Place all dominoes face down. Each player picks the same number of dominoes. According to traditional rules, each player should start with 7, but if the children are very young, start with 4. The dominoes that have not been picked by the players become the reserve pile. The youngest player starts by placing a domino face up on the table. The next player must match one of his dominoes with one of the designs of the domino on the table. If he does so, his turn is over. If a player is unable to play because he fails to have a matching domino, he must draw from the reserve pile. He must continue to draw until he can play a matching domino. If a player is unable to play and no dominoes remain in the reserve pile, he must pass. The first player to use up all his dominoes wins.

28

Trampoline

Allowing your child to jump on a pillow or mat placed on the floor is a good alternative to having him jump on your bed. Mom and Dad, this is a good time to dust off the exercise trampoline that you've had for years and used only once! This activity is especially fun if the child can see himself jumping in a mirror placed at a safe distance.

> **Caution:** Trampolines can be dangerous if jumping is not supervised.

29

Stringing

Have your child create a personalized belt, headband, or necklace by stringing painted spools, Cheerios, Fruit Loops, or macaroni on an extra-long shoelace, string, or piece of yarn. The macaroni can be dyed by dipping it quickly in a mixture of tap water and food coloring. Use four drops of coloring for every one cup of water and make sure to allow the macaroni to dry before stringing it.

30

Puzzles

Construct homemade puzzles by gluing magazine pictures, greeting cards, or photos to cardboard or construction paper. Cut the reinforced picture into as many pieces as are appropriate for the age of your child (toddlers can handle four pieces; preschoolers, six to ten pieces). For a variation, collect family photos that are nearly the same size. Glue each picture to different colored pieces of construction paper. Then, cut each picture into four equal pieces. Your child can either mix and match the pieces, making new pictures, or he can use the color backing as a guide to putting the original photos back together.

31

Gluing Craft

Your child can glue assorted items such as macaroni, beans, popped corn, felt, or fabric on heavy paper or a paper plate. Use a cupcake tin or egg carton to keep these items sorted. Use the following recipe for an easy glue.

∎ **GLUE RECIPE** ∎

Combine the following:

¹/₄ cup flour   *¹/₄ cup milk*

32

Sewing Cards

Draw a bold picture or design on a lightweight piece of cardboard and make holes along the design's outline with a hand-held paper punch. Show your child how to lace a long shoelace or thick piece of yarn through the holes as though he is sewing. When the sewing is finished, the yarn will create a picture.

33

Bake and Paint Sculpture

 If you would like to save your child's first sculptural attempts, have her use this bake and paint clay.

▮ BAKE AND PAINT CLAY RECIPE ▮

4 cups flour　　　　　　*1½ cups water*
1 cup salt

Mix ingredients. Once your child has finished her sculpture, place it on a cookie sheet and bake at 350° until it is dry, but not brown. Baking time will vary depending on the size of the sculpture. Let it cool before painting. For paint, see Basic Paint Recipe (activity #61), or use store-bought tempera paint.

34

Starch and Tissue Paper Collage

Tear, crumple, or cut apart sheets of tissue paper of various colors. Using a medium-size paintbrush, cover the surface of a piece of construction paper with a thin layer of liquid laundry starch (found at the grocery store). Let your child apply the tissue paper to the wet surface to create a colorful collage.

A stained glass window can be made using one variation of this activity. Brush a layer of starch across a 12 x 12-inch piece of wax paper. Apply various colored 1 x 1-inch tissue paper squares to the starch. Brush a second layer of starch over the tissue paper. Finish the window by placing a second 12 x 12-inch piece of wax paper over the collage. This project is best displayed in a window.

Caution: Starch should not be eaten.

35

Simple Scissor Craft

Save magazine inserts or any heavyweight paper. This type of paper is easier for the young child learning to use scissors to manipulate. Once your child has mastered cutting skills, she will enjoy looking through magazines to identify and cut out numbers, the alphabet, zoo and farm animals, body parts, and colors. Any of these can be grouped into categories and pasted on paper.

Caution: Always use blunt safety scissors made for small children.

36

Kiddie Correspondence

Keep a stream of artwork going from grandchild to grandparent. This activity will occupy your child and make the grandparents happy, too. Start the habit of writing thank-you notes for birthday and Christmas gifts by having your child color a picture; write a short note on it and if the child is able, have him sign his name.

37

Junk Mail

Some great activities can be derived from junk mail. Let your child play with unopened, discarded mail while you are paying the bills. This will occupy your child while you concentrate on your paperwork.

Keep all the stamps and stickers found in advertisements for use in future art projects. Also hold onto old catalogs, particularly those with pictures of toys or young children. Your child will enjoy browsing through them, which will in turn give you some time to look at a magazine or your favorite store's catalog.

Allow your child to play mailman with unopened junk mail. Place letters in a sack and deliver to post office boxes made from shoe boxes or oatmeal boxes. Remove lids from boxes or cut slots, leaving a place for the mail to be inserted. Rain, sleet, or snow is not required for this activity!

38

Memory Book

After a special day at the zoo, beach, or park, have your child draw several pictures of the day's events. Add photos and printed souvenirs if appropriate. Staple or tie loose pages together with yarn to bind into a memory book.

39

Personalized Photo Album

Have you always wondered what to do with those less-than-perfect photographs of your child? Put them in a photo album with pages that have a transparent adhesive covering that wipes off easily. Your child will enjoy spending time looking through the different pictures.

40

Musical Instruments

 Turn ordinary household items into musical instruments.

- Shakers: Fill plastic medicine bottles or margarine tubs with beans, macaroni, or beads. Secure the lids with glue or electrical tape.
- Cymbals: Two pot lids.
- Drums: Coffee cans, oatmeal boxes, large plastic tubs, plastic bleach or milk bottles.
- Drumsticks: Use wooden spoons or rubber spatulas.
- Guitar: Rubber bands wrapped around an empty tissue box.
- Horns: Punch holes down the length of an empty toilet paper, paper towel, or wrapping paper roll.
- Harmonica: Wrap a comb in a wax paper.

If your child has friends over—or if you have a few children of your own—you can have your own marching band.

MUSICAL INSTRUMENTS

41

Homemade Cassette Tape

When making your own cassette tapes, record sounds and activities that will cater to your own child's interests. Here are some ideas.

- A familiar voice singing nursery rhymes and favorite songs
- Participatory activities such as "Simon Says" or the "Hokey Pokey"
- Favorite animal and transportation sounds
- Favorite stories read by a parent or a grandparent

A babysitter can use this tape if your child misses you and needs to hear your voice.

42

Personalized Video

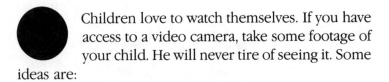 Children love to watch themselves. If you have access to a video camera, take some footage of your child. He will never tire of seeing it. Some ideas are:

- Dancing to music
- Playing musical instruments (see activity #40)
- Birthday parties
- Visits from friends and relatives
- Holiday celebrations
- Special school events
- Amusement parks and zoos

43

Toy Pick-up Time

It is never too early to teach your child to put away her toys. If she can throw a toy, she can put it away. Make a game out of it and participate with her. Establish a time each day to pick up toys. Place assorted toy containers throughout the house to save steps.

Outdoor Play

44

Sidewalk Painting

On a warm day allow your child to "paint" with an old paintbrush and a container of water on your sidewalks, patios, and fences. When the artist's work is finished, the sun will take care of the clean-up.

45

Chalk Graffiti

Create outdoor murals on paved areas with white or colored chalk. If there is more than one child playing, have them take turns tracing around each other's bodies. The chalk is easily removed by washing it away with "sidewalk painting" (see activity #44).

Caution: Toddlers can choke on small pieces of chalk if swallowed. We recommend using dustless chalk, which can be found in educational toy stores.

46

Lawn Bowling

Save large plastic bottles to use as bowling pins. Have your child line them up and attempt to knock them down by rolling a large heavyweight ball, such as a soccer ball or basketball, toward the pins. On a windy day, you may want to fill the bottles with 2 or 3 inches of water or sand.

47

Ice Castles

This is a fun project for a summer day. Fill several empty milk cartons, frozen juice cans, and ice cream tubs with water. Freeze overnight or until solid. Just prior to starting the activity, peel away the cartons and expose the blocks of ice. Outside, stack the different shapes of ice in a big tub (with the largest blocks at the base) to form the castle. Your child will now enjoy dripping various colors of food dye and sprinkling pinches of rock salt (found at the grocery store) over the ice. The rock salt will bond the blocks of ice together and help the food coloring to penetrate the ice. Your child will be proud of her colorful summertime sculpture longer than it will last!

Caution: This activity is *messy*! We suggest it be done in a grassy area.

48

Bubbles

Making bubbles is a great source of self-amusement. Shape large homemade wands from wire coat hangers, making sure to wind any stray ends around the main wire and also to bind any sharp points with electrical tape. Have your child dip the wand in a large container, such as a frying pan or bucket, filled with bubble soap (see recipe below). These big loops will create oversize bubbles.

A steady stream of bubbles can be generated by holding a wand in front of a small electric fan. This technique will need to be supervised to make sure *only* the bubbles get in the way of the fan.

A variety of inexpensive accessories can be purchased at a toy store. Bubble pipes are a good introduction for young toddlers who are unable to blow through the wand.

■ BUBBLE RECIPE ■

Combine the following:

*½ cup Dawn or Joy
dishwashing liquid
(brands found to
work best)
8 cups water*

*2 tablespoons glycerine
(optional—found in
drugstore)
A pinch of sugar (to
bind)*

49

Water Play

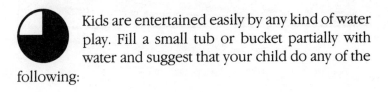 Kids are entertained easily by any kind of water
play. Fill a small tub or bucket partially with
water and suggest that your child do any of the
following:

- Give a babydoll a bath
- Sail plastic boats
- Wash unbreakable dishes

Add a dash of soap to the tub and use a hand egg beater
to whip up some suds.

50

Toddler Boot Camp

 Give your child a challenge by setting up an outdoor obstacle course using any combination of the following:

- A tire or ladder lying flat
- Heavy beams and boards to place on boxes for ramps and bridges
- A sawhorse
- A barrel
- Large boxes

Caution: For safety purposes, keep in mind your child's coordination skills when setting up the course.

TODDLER BOOT CAMP

51

Tire Swings

A tire is an inexpensive and space-saving alternative to a swing set. By attaching a tire to a tree with rope or chain, your child can sit in it, stand on it, spin in it, or swing. (It helps to drill a hole in the bottom of the tire so that rain water can drain out.)

52

Grand Prix

Construct a raceway for tricycles, toy cars, or wagons by using plastic liter-size bottles filled with sand as pylons. Your child will now enjoy weaving in, out, and around the bottles.

53

Under Construction

Line up and tape together a group of medium-size open-ended cardboard boxes to form a tunnel. Your child will spend a great deal of time crawling through the structure. Use a larger box (appliance-size) to construct a fort, house, or high-rise building. Cut openings to create doors and windows. Flags, child-size furniture, sheets, and blankets will add the finishing touches.

54

Pit Stop

Create a gas station. A tree can serve as the pump, a jump rope with a handle becomes a gas hose and a nozzle, and a tricycle makes a fine car. An entrepreneurial child will offer discounts to those who pay cash.

55

Car Wash

Your child will enjoy helping you wash your car. Provide a bucket, rag, or spray bottle to be used in a designated area. Alternatively, an outing to the car wash is an exciting field trip for a young child.

56

Butterfly Net

Form a circle at the end of a wire hanger; leave approximately half of the wire for a handle. Secure the circle by twisting the base of the handle, and wrap all sharp edges with electrical tape. Use a lightweight sock or a leg from an ultra-sheer pair of pantyhose, cut at the knee, as a net. Wrap the raw edges of the sock or nylon net around the wire hanger circle and hand stitch a small hem to encase the wire hanger. Your child will now be ready to catch all those creatures you don't want in the house.

57

Nature Collage

After a walk, have you ever had trouble convincing your child to leave those collected treasures behind? Instead of trying, make a collage by pasting the collection (leaves, sticks, flowers, etc.) to construction paper. Use the recipe for paste below:

▌ PASTE RECIPE ▌

¹/₂ cup flour
¹/₂ cup white sugar
*¹/₂ tablespoon
  powdered alum
  (from drugstore)*

¹/₂ cup cold water
¹/₂ cup boiling water

Combine flour, sugar, alum, and cold water. Mix well. Add boiling water. Then, heat the ingredients in the top of a double boiler, stirring constantly until thick and clear. Let cool. Store in an airtight container.

58

Birdwatching

Kids enjoy watching birds. Help them with their search for new species by providing them with a pair of toy binoculars. To make binoculars, tape two empty toilet paper rolls together side by side. If your child wishes to wear them, attach a ribbon, which can be loosely tied around the neck. Now your child is all set to conduct nature walks in his very own backyard.

59

Rock Collecting

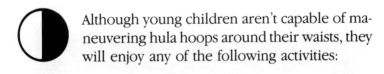 Select a box or sack in which to keep rocks that your child finds on outdoor expeditions. She will enjoy sorting them later, as she adds to the collection (and not, we hope, throwing them through your windows).

60

Hula Hoops

Although young children aren't capable of maneuvering hula hoops around their waists, they will enjoy any of the following activities:

∎ Rolling or spinning the hoop
∎ Jumping in and out of the hoop
∎ Sitting in the hoop and racing small vehicles around the outside
∎ Tossing unbreakable objects into a stationary hoop (see Bean Bag, activity #13)

61

General Painting

Save old baby food jars to use as paint containers. An old shirt makes an excellent smock. Always use water-soluble paint or the following recipe. Liquid soap can also be mixed into the paint for easy cleanup. If you feel that your child is still a bit young for brush or finger painting, purchase a paint-with-water book. The book will create its own paint when the child applies a wet brush to the page and will also eliminate some of the cleanup.

Each of the activities described in numbers 61 through 68 should occupy your child for about an hour.

■ BASIC PAINT RECIPE ■

1 tablespoon sugar
½ cup corn starch
¾ cup cold water
2 cups boiling water

food coloring
1 tablespoon liquid
soap (optional)

Combine sugar, cornstarch, and cold water in sauce pan. Mix well. Pour boiling water into the mixture, stirring as you pour. Cook over medium heat. Stir constantly until thick and clear. Allow the mixture to cool and then divide into separate containers. Add a different color food coloring to each container.

Caution: Painting is messy. Your child may do any of the following activities inside; however, we recommend that painting be done outdoors.

62

Blow Painting

Using an eyedropper, place several drops of nontoxic paint on a sheet of paper. Your child should then blow through a straw held close to the paint. The paint will spread on the paper, causing a splattered effect.

63

Roller Painting

Use a roll-on deodorant bottle as a paint applicator. Remove the roller, wash out the bottle, and then pour in paint. Then replace the roller. Or, your child can dip the end of the roller into the paint and apply it directly to paper.

64

Marble Painting

Place a piece of paper in the bottom of a shallow cardboard box. Put approximately 1 tablespoon of paint in the middle of the paper. Place one or more marbles in the box. Have your child tilt the box back and forth. The marbles will roll through the paint, making streaks of color on the paper.

65

Stamp Painting

You child can dip food and household items in paint and apply to paper to create innovative patterns. Make a stamp by slicing open a vegetable to form a flat surface. Carve or dig a design into the vegetable's flat surface. Appropriate fruits or vegetables for this activity are potatoes, turnips, and apples. The natural texture of other vegetables such as cabbage will form its own unique pattern. Curlers, furniture casters, and various kitchen utensils can also be used.

66

Sponge Painting

Cut a sponge into 1-inch squares. You can also purchase precut bath sponges in various animal shapes. Using one sponge for each color of paint, show your child how to dab the sponge onto the painting surface and create his own design.

67

String Painting

Have your child dip string into paint and apply to the surface of paper using any of the following methods:

- Hold string with clothespins while dipping in paint; then apply directly to paper.
- Place paint-covered string inside of a folded piece of paper. Have your child place one hand on top of the folded paper while he removes the string by pulling from the side. Unfold the paper to reveal a painted design.
- Wrap thick string around an empty paper towel roll. Dip in paint and roll on the surface of the paper.

68

Painted Spaghetti Art

Overcook a small portion of spaghetti and drain. Have your child apply the spaghetti to a piece of construction paper. Once dried, it will stick to the paper, forming a raised design. Your child will enjoy painting the textured surface.

69

Yard Work

Your child will enjoy playing in the garden. He can actually help by picking up leaves or sweeping with a small broom. Inexpensive toy yard tools made of plastic, such as hoes, rakes, and lawn mowers, are also available.

70

Flower Garden

When pruning back flowers and shrubs, give your child the cuttings. Have him place the cuttings in a pot or small area of soil, creating his own temporary garden. For safety's sake, avoid any possibly poisonous plants or plants with thorns.

71

Magnet Magic

 Your child will enjoy conducting scientific experiments while doing any of the following activities:

- Show your child how to drag a magnet through the sand to collect black particles of iron.
- Give your child an assortment of metal and non-metal objects and let her see which items will stick to a magnet.
- Cut out fish shapes from construction paper, approximately 3 inches long. Slide a large paper clip on the head end of each fish. Attach a small horseshoe magnet to a stick with an 8- to 12-inch string. Your child can now go fishing.

These activities will give you an opportunity to explain how magnets attract metal.

72

Picnic Lunch

If you want to spend an afternoon outside, pack a picnic lunch and bring a blanket. Include a wet wash rag wrapped in plastic for washing hands before lunch. When your child becomes hungry and tired, have her lay out her blanket and eat lunch. Afterward, she can nap, which will leave you free to enjoy the *quiet* of the outdoors. Bring a book or magazine!

Around Town

73

Personalized Road Map

On a heavyweight piece of paper, draw a simple map of places that you visit frequently. Along the route identify your child's favorite places by pasting pictures or drawing symbols to represent the location of grandparents, friends, the grocery store, the local shopping mall, the doctor's office, and especially your own home. Fold the map so that your child can open it easily, and keep it in an accessible spot in the car. Your child will enjoy finding your travel destination on his own map.

74

Personalized Travel Tape

Make a special tape for your child which can be played on your car stereo. One side can be her favorite songs or sounds. The other side can be soft music or lullabies sung by a favorite person such as Grandma; this side can be used when your child needs to wind down, or when it's nap time.

75

Toy Organizer

Purchase a toy organizer that fits over the head rest of your car and hangs over the back of the seat. Made of large pockets, these organizers provide easily accessible storage space for toys.

76

Travel Photo Album

Fill a photo album that has pages with a transparent adhesive covering with pictures of some of your child's favorite things: puppies, babies, toys, and family members. The slick pages will wipe clean and pictures can be added or rearranged easily. The book *can* be kept permanently in the car and used as a special treat when you are traveling.

TOY ORGANIZER

77

Tour Guide

 When traveling with your child, point out the many interesting kinds of vehicles and places that will interest him.

- Trucks/buses
- Helicopters/airplanes
- Road work/construction work
- Postal trucks/fire engines and firehouses
- Holiday decorations/Christmas lights
- Colors/numbers

Eventually your child will become your own personal tour guide, pointing out everything in view.

78

Cloth Activity Book

Fabric, felt, buttons, and thread can be used to make a simple activity book for your child. For pages, cut six to eight rectangles measuring 8 x 12 inches from a piece of fabric. It's a good idea to use pinking shears on the edges of each page to keep them from unraveling. Stack the rectangles and sew a seam along one side to form a binding. Sew large buttons on each page. A variety of colors and shapes will make it more fun. On separate pieces of felt, cut out various shapes such as flowers, triangles, circles, or animals. Cut slits in the center of each shape to form a buttonhole. Your child can now button the shapes into the book. Challenge his imagination by encouraging him to create stories by rearranging the shapes throughout the book.

79

Sports Fans

When the family goes to a sporting event, one way to occupy your little athlete during the game is to have her bring her own pair of binoculars (see Birdwatching, activity #58). Another is allowing her to listen to the game on the radio with a headset. Make sure that the volume is set properly before placing the headset on your child. Small toys, crayons, and paper can be brought out when your child loses interest in her surroundings. When all else fails, bring on the hot dogs!

80

Restaurant Dining

Taking your child to a restaurant can be a real "event." Bring plastic utensils for the child who likes to attract attention by banging the silverware on the table. Save yourself the embarrassment of spills by bringing along a nonspill cup. Bring crayons and coloring books or use the paper place mats for artwork. Children can become very hungry before the meal is served, so order crackers or bread right away, or bring your own snacks. A "surprise package" of small toys can also be brought out when times get tough. *Bon appétit!*

81

Grocery Shopping

Always feed your child before going grocery shopping because your child will tend to say "I want" more often when she is hungry. Your grocery list or coupons can be used to occupy your child's "busy" hands while she rides in the shopping cart, but be prepared to pick up discarded coupons. Involving your child in your selections and maintaining a constant flow of conversation will keep her entertained. After taking a two-year-old to the market regularly, you'll be amazed at how much can be said about a head of lettuce.

82

Mall Shopping

If you are going to be shopping for a long period of time, you will find it easier to restrain your child by keeping him in a stroller. Coax your child into the stroller by bringing along a cassette player and tapes. When possible, park your stroller in front of a nearby mirror or an interesting display while you browse. If your child is old enough, he will enjoy pushing his own stroller through the mall. When he becomes fussy, take a break and give him your full attention. If you find that you are stopping frequently, it's time to go home.

83

Food to Go

There are now many nutritious snacks packaged in convenient sizes for travel. Fruit juices come in boxes with straws attached. Raisins, dried fruit snacks, toddler crackers, small cereal boxes, and even apple sauce and puddings are packaged in individual servings. These items can be purchased and kept in a diaper or travel bag for future "emergency" situations. Although these individually packaged servings can be expensive, their convenience makes them worth it when all else fails!

Special Occasions

84

Custom Birthday Invitations

Have your child join in the preparation for her own birthday party by making the invitations. Here are some ideas for items that your child can paste on the card:

- To illustrate the theme of the party, cut out appropriate pictures from magazines.
- To represent the child's age, cut out numbers.
- To decorate the invitations, use recycled pieces of wrapping paper and ribbon.
- To add an extra-festive touch, sprinkle confetti or glitter over any of the above invitation ideas.

85

Pretend Birthday Parties

Kids love birthday parties, especially their own. Since it's difficult for your child to celebrate only once a year, he will enjoy holding imaginary parties for friends, family, dolls, and stuffed animals. Baking pretend cakes, blowing out candles, singing "Happy Birthday," and wrapping and opening play gifts will help him to relive the excitement of his own special day.

86

Personalized Valentines

We find that friends and relatives are especially charmed by homemade Valentines. Cut red or pink construction paper into heart shapes, or simply make a card by folding the paper. Have your child glue on a combination of any of the following:

- Sequins
- Lace or doilies
- Yarn or ribbon
- Small pictures of your child
- Stickers or cut-out hearts
- Dried flowers
- Wrapping paper or old greeting card pictures

87

Easter Thumbprint Creatures

Your child can make bunnies, chicks, and other animals by using an ink pad and her thumb. Have your child press her thumb onto the ink pad and then apply to paper. Apply whiskers, ears, beaks, feathers—or whatever—with a pen or marker. It's best to use a water-base ink pad; its traces will more readily come off skin and clothing. These critters make great cards and decorations for Easter.

88

May Day Baskets

Create a May Day Basket by attaching a pipe cleaner handle to an empty strawberry box. Your child can now decorate the container by weaving ribbon, yarn, or narrow strips of pastel construction paper through the lattice. Fill the basket with fresh flowers or other items gathered on your springtime walks.

89

Mother's Day Jewelry

Make clay according to the recipe for bake and paint clay (see Bake and Paint Sculpture, activity #33). To make beads for a necklace, form small balls. Before baking, use a toothpick to make a hole in each bead large enough for stringing. Your child can paint the baked beads various colors and string to the desired length (see Basic Paint, activity #61).

90

Father's Day Tie

Father's Day wouldn't be complete without giving Dad the traditional tie. With a discarded toothbrush, allow your child to apply fabric paint to a new or used solid-color tie. This is not a tie that will need to go to the cleaners often—spots of spaghetti sauce, catsup, and mustard will only add to its artistic composition.

91

Fourth of July Parade

 Create your own parade with family and friends. Here are some suggestions.

- Attach streamers to tricycles and wagons.
- Play loud patriotic music.
- Form a band (see Musical Instruments, activity #40).
- Carry a flag.
- Dress in red, white, and blue.
- Everyone must wear a hat!

92

Haunted House

Make a haunted house by taping together large appliance boxes. Line up open-ended smaller boxes to form an entrance or exit. Place blankets, foam, or mats on the floor to make it more comfortable to crawl through. Paint or paste pumpkin faces, friendly witches, and ghosts to the inside walls. Place small carved pumpkins and orange and black streamers inside the haunted house. Use Halloween music or spooky sounds to provide a little more atmosphere. When decorating the interior, keep the age of your child and her fears in mind.

93

Ghost

In anticipation of Halloween, your child will enjoy playing ghost in her very own backyard. Take a sheet and cut out holes for eyes. After placing the sheet over your child's head, cut away the extra fabric along the bottom. Now your "little monster" will temporarily disappear.

94

Thanksgiving Indian Headdress

Cut a strip of construction paper 1 inch wide. Place this around your child's head and tape to fit. Use real feathers or make your own from construction paper. Glue or tape the feathers to the back of the headdress. Use the following recipe to paint your child's face.

∎ FACE PAINT RECIPE ∎

1¼ teaspoon
    cornstarch
½ teaspoon water
1¼ teaspoon cold
    cream
1 drop food coloring

Mix all ingredients together with a popsicle stick or chopstick. Use a muffin tin to separate colors. Apply the paint to your child's face with your fingers.

Now all he needs is a tom-tom (see Musical Instruments, activity #40).

95

Wrapping Paper Play

Use recycled gift wrap and ribbon for art projects or for your child to wrap pretend gifts. This is a good way to keep your child busy while you are wrapping gifts at holiday time.

96

Cookie Cutter Cards

Make Christmas or Hanukkah cards by dipping appropriately shaped cookie cutters in paint and applying to construction paper. Sprinkle glitter over the wet paint to add a little sparkle.

97

Holiday Wrapping Paper

Here are a couple of ideas for creating your holiday wrapping. For Hanukkah, let your child apply the side of a dreidel dipped in blue, silver, gold, or white paint to paper. (See activity #61 for Basic Paint Recipe or use nontoxic water-base paint.) For Christmas, cut a candy cane shape from corrugated cardboard. Strip off one side of the cardboard to expose the corrugated texture. Use the shape as a stamp by brushing it with red or green paint and applying it to the paper.

98

Tissue Paper Wreath

Your child can make a Christmas wreath by using a paper plate, colored tissue paper, liquid starch (found at the grocery store), and ribbon. Cut out and discard the center of the paper plate, leaving a 1½-inch edge. Cut the tissue paper into 2-inch squares and allow your child to crumple each individual piece. Evenly apply starch to the paper-plate wreath base with a paintbrush. The tissue paper can now be stuck onto the plate. Puncture a hole at the edge of the wreath, and tie a bright ribbon through it to use as a hanger.

> **Caution:** Starch should not be eaten.

99

Holiday Crayon Cookies

Recycle old crayon stubs by making them into variegated holiday crayon cookies. Remove paper from crayons and break into small pieces no bigger than ½ inch. Fill baking tins halfway with a variety of different colored crayons. Use muffin tins or small holiday baking molds such as Christmas trees, Santa faces, etc., which can be found in catalogs or cookware stores. Bake in the oven on the lowest setting for 10 to 15 minutes. Remove from the oven just before the crayons start to liquefy. Allow to cool before removing from tin. These colorful crayon cookies can now be wrapped and given as homemade holiday gifts or party favors.

> **Caution:** These "cookies" are not edible. Also, keep children away from a hot oven.

100

Santa Play

This is a fun way to remember Santa's visit over and over again. Give your child a pillow case to use as Santa's toy bag. He will enjoy filling it with toys and pretending to be Santa making holiday deliveries.

101

New Year's Eve Celebration

Before putting your child to bed on New Year's Eve, make time for a pint-size celebration. Pull out your pots and pans for noisemakers. If you want to have your own Times Square party, you can also use hats, blowers, or streamers. Let your child welcome the New Year by making as much noise as possible!

Activity Index

Bake and Paint Sculpture, 31
Bathtub Painting, 4
Bean Bags, 15
Birdwatching, 52
Blow Painting, 55
Bubbles, 44
Butterfly Net, 50
Car Wash, 49
Chalk, 20
Chalk Graffiti, 41
Cloth Activity Book, 68
Cookie Cutter Cards, 83
Cook's Assistant, 9
Crayon Rubbings, 21
Custom Birthday Invitations, 75
Dishwashing, 11
Dominoes, 26
Dress-up, 25
Easter Thumbprint Creatures, 77
Fake Finger Painting, 3
Father's Day Tie, 78
Flower Garden, 60
Food to Go, 72
Fourth of July Parade, 79
General Crayon, 21
General Painting, 54
Ghost, 81
Gluing Craft, 29
Grand Prix, 48
Grocery Shopping, 70
Hair Salon, 24
Hand Puppets, 14
Haunted House, 80
Holiday Crayon Cookies, 85
Holiday Wrapping Paper, 84
Homemade Cassette Tape, 37
Homemade Playdough, 6
Housekeeping, 11

Hula Hoops, 53
Ice Castles, 43
Indoor Sandbox, 3
Junk Mail, 34
Kiddie Correspondence, 33
Laundry Basket Play, 23
Lawn Bowling, 42
Life-size Doll, 16
Magic Etchings, 22
Magnet Magic, 61
Mall Shopping, 71
Marble Painting, 56
Masking Tape Highways, 12
Masks, 13
May Day Baskets, 77
Memory Book, 35
Mother's Day Jewelry, 78
Musical Instruments, 36
Nature Collage, 51
New Year's Eve Celebration, 86
Obstacle Course, 18
Painted Spaghetti Art, 58
Paper Bag Blocks, 16
Personalized Photo Album, 35
Personalized Road Map, 65
Personalized Travel Tape, 65

Personalized Valentines, 76
Personalized Video, 38
Picnic Lunch, 62
Pit Stop, 49
Play Kitchens, 8
Pretend Birthday Parties, 75
Puzzles, 28
Resist Painting, 22
Restaurant Dining, 70
Robot Play, 17
Rock Collecting, 53
Roller Painting, 56
Santa Play, 86
Sewing Cards, 30
Sidewalk Painting, 41
Simple Scissor Craft, 33
Sponge Painting, 57
Sports Fan, 69
Stamp Painting, 57
Starch and Tissue Paper Collage, 32
String Painting, 58
Stringing, 28
Table Setting, 10
Tent, 19
Thanksgiving Indian Headdress, 82
Tire Swings, 47
Tissue Paper Wreath, 84
Toddler Boot Camp, 46
Tour Guide, 67

Toy Organizer, 66
Toy Pick-up Time, 38
Trampoline, 27
Travel Photo Album, 66

Under Construction, 48
Water Play, 45
Wrapping Paper Play, 83
Yard Work, 59

Recipe Index

Each recipe appears once in the book, as indicated by the page numbers following each entry in this index. The sub-entries are subsequent activities that refer to the recipes.

Bake and Paint Clay, 31
  Bake and Paint Sculpture, 31
  Mother's Day Jewelry, 78

Basic Paint, 54
  Blow Painting, 55
  Holiday Wrapping Paper, 84
  Marble Painting, 56
  Mother's Day Jewelry, 78
  Painted Spaghetti Art, 58
  Resist Painting, 22
  Roller Painting, 56
  Sponge Painting, 57
  Stamp Painting, 57
  String Painting, 58

Bubbles, 44

Face Paint, 82
  Dress-up, 25
  Thanksgiving Indian Headdress, 82

Finger Paint, 5
  Bathtub Painting, 4

Glue, 29
  Gluing Craft, 29
  Puzzles, 28

Homemade Playdough, 6
  Cook's Assistant, 9
  Play Kitchens, 8

Paste, 51
    Custom Birthday Invita-
        tions, 75
    Dominoes, 26
    Hand Puppets, 14
    Masks, 13
    Nature Collage, 51

Personalized Road Map,
    65
Personalized Valentines,
    76
Robot Play, 17
Simple Scissor Craft, 35